HAPPY NEW YEAR

COLORING

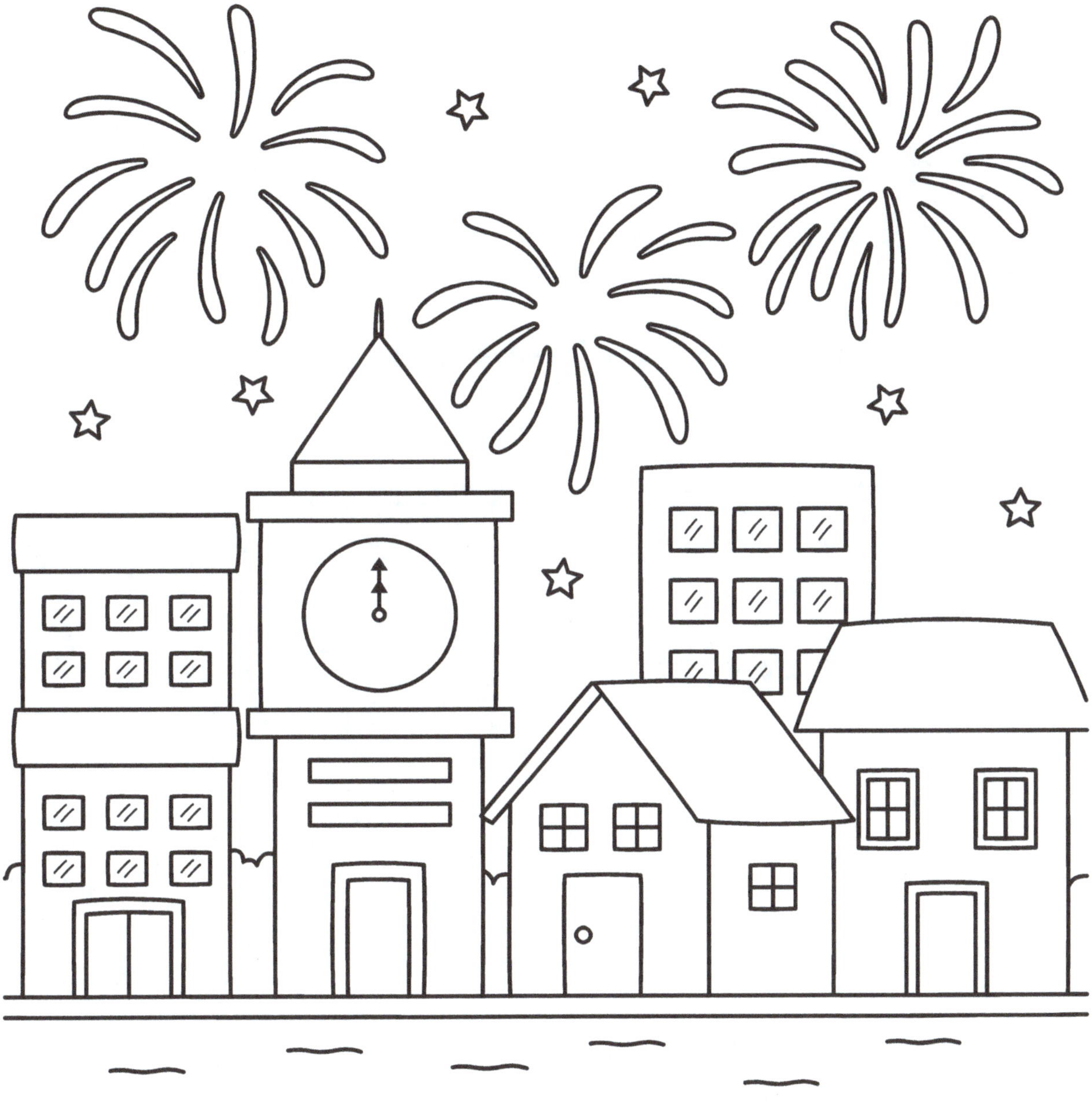

HAVE A PROSPEROUS YEAR AHEAD!

HAPPY NEW YEAR
COLORING

HAVE A PROSPEROUS YEAR AHEAD!

HAPPY NEW YEAR
COLORING

HAVE A PROSPEROUS YEAR AHEAD!

Merry Christmas!

Happy New Year

HAPPY NEW YEAR
WORD SEARCH

Find and circle the words.

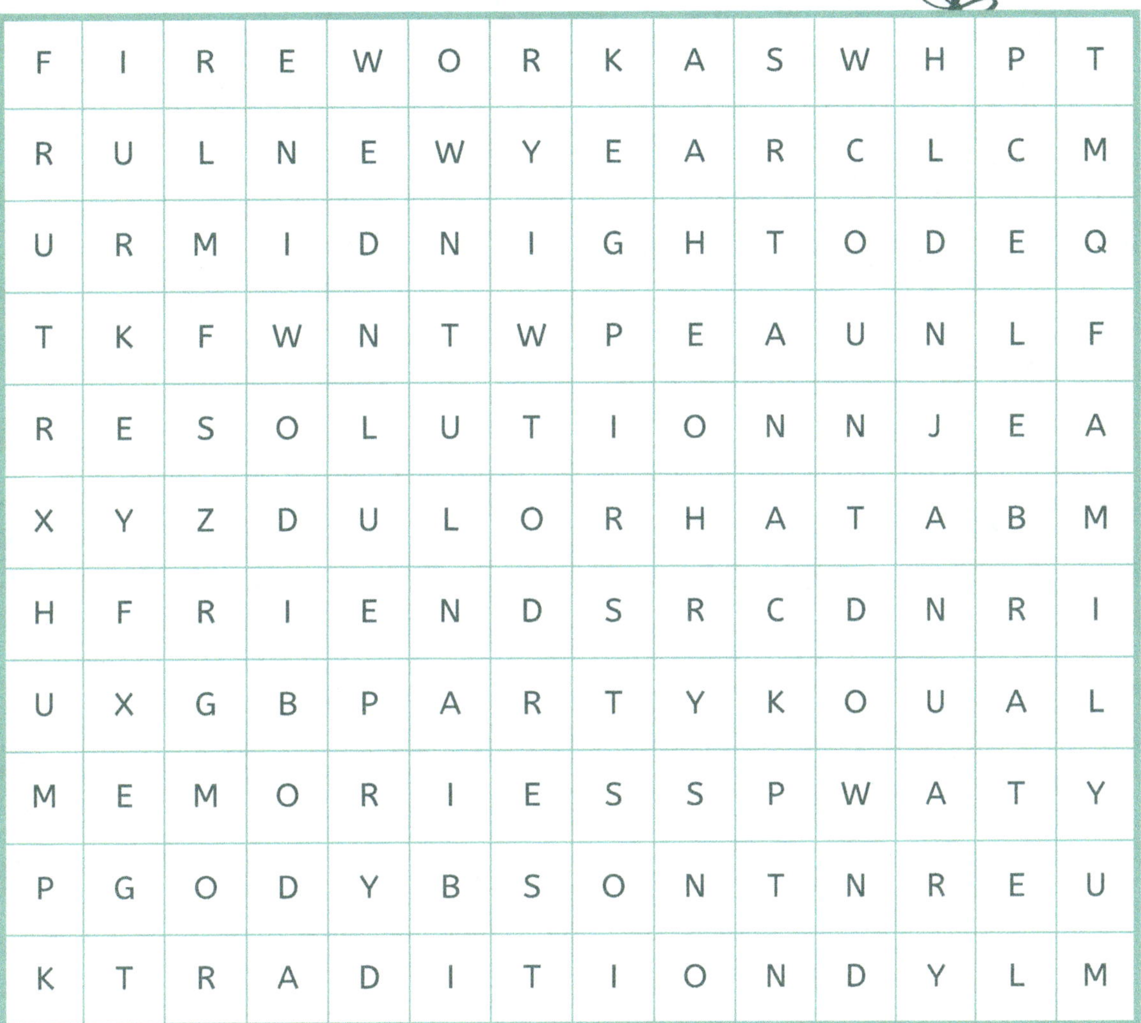

Firework	Party	New Year
Midnight	Family	Celebrate
Tradition	Friends	Resolution
Memories	January	Countdown

New Year Word Search

Circle words in the puzzle below

```
F  E  S  T  I  V  A  L  T
I  A  N  L  Y  H  P  U  I
R  D  R  A  G  O  N  N  G
E  A  S  N  L  L  R  A  E
W  N  W  T  U  E  R  R  R
O  C  S  E  C  D  D  C  L
R  E  O  R  K  A  E  A  I
K  U  S  N  O  Y  T  R  O
E  N  V  E  L  O  P  E  N
```

lunar	tiger	lion	lantern
festival	dragon	dance	red
firework	holiday	luck	envelope

NEW YEAR
Postcard

Fill in the postcard, cut out and send.

Dear ....,

....

....

....

....

Best, ...

CHRISTMAS
MAZE PUZZLE

Christmas
Word Search

Find the words below in the word search.

A	S	S	L	E	I	G	H	B	C	C	O
U	A	T	R	P	J	I	H	F	O	D	R
S	N	O	W	M	A	N	N	G	O	E	N
T	T	C	Q	A	O	N	M	L	K	C	A
V	A	K	D	B	C	G	I	W	I	A	M
R	E	I	N	D	E	E	R	R	E	N	E
G	I	N	G	E	R	B	R	E	A	D	N
W	Y	G	A	E	F	H	J	A	L	Y	T
X	Z	M	I	S	T	L	E	T	O	E	Q
C	H	I	M	N	E	Y	K	H	M	N	P

SANTA	CHIMNEY	SLEIGH
REINDEER	GINGERBREAD	MISTLETOE
SNOWMAN	ORNAMENT	CANDY
STOCKING	WREATH	COOKIE

CHRISTMAS
MAZE PUZZLE

Name: _______________   Date: __________

Instruction: Help penguin find its way to the truck to take the Christmas tree home.

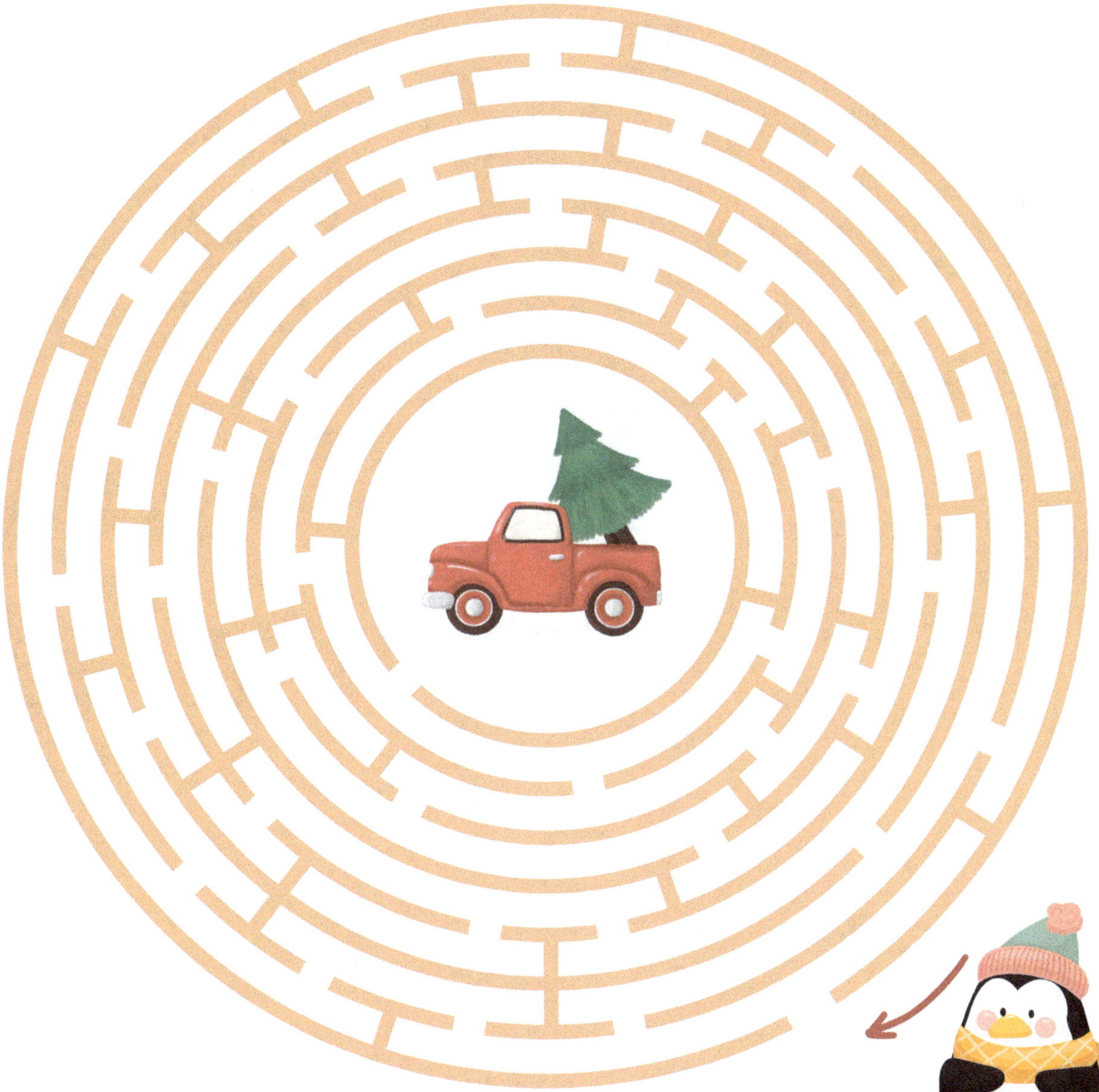

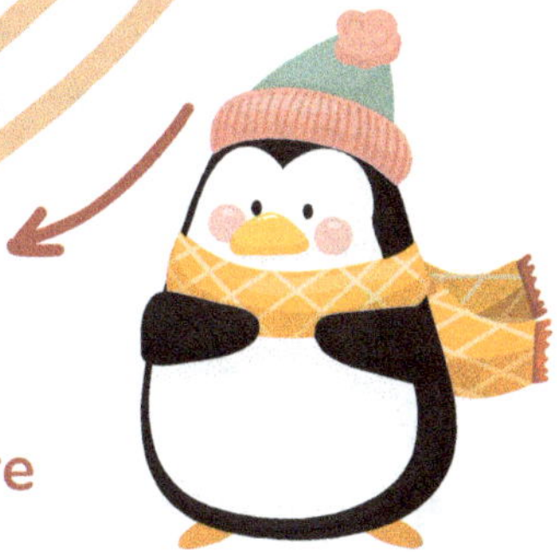

CHRISTMAS MAZE PUZZLE

Instruction: Help Santa find his way to the houses to have more cookies.

Start here

I SPY CHRISTMAS

Count the Christmas-themed items in the box and write the amount in the blanks given below.

Roll and color

Roll the dice and color the Christmas elements.

Color by Number

Use the color key below.

Color by Number

Use the color key below.

Christmas Tracing

Trace the lines.

CHRISTMAS TRACING ACTIVITY

Trace the line for each character

WORKSHEET
CHRISTMAS ADDITION

NAME :   GRADE :

Can you add the christmas pictures?

= 4   = 3   = 2   = 1

1. + + =

2. + + =

3. + + =

4. + + =

CHRISTMAS COUNTING

Count and circle the correct number.

| 2 | 3 | 4 |

| 1 | 2 | 3 |

| 5 | 6 | 7 |

| 7 | 8 | 9 |

| 4 | 5 | 6 |

| 6 | 7 | 8 |

FIND THE SHADOW

Draw a line from the object to the correct shadow.

Find the Differences - Christmas

Can you find 5 differences in these two pictures?

Find the Differences

Find five differences in these two pictures.